The Last Canadian to Kiss the Pope's Ring

Written by
Katie Turner, Austin Mardon, & Catherine Mardon

Copyright © 2021 by Austin Mardon
All rights reserved. This book or any portion thereof may not be reproduced or used in any manner whatsoever without the express written permission of the publisher except for the use of brief quotations in a book review or scholarly journal.
First Printing: 2021

Typeset and Cover Design by Kim Huynh

ISBN: 978-1-77369-656-0
EBook ISBN: 978-1-77369-657-7

Golden Meteorite Press
103 11919 82 St NW
Edmonton, AB T5B 2W3
www.goldenmeteoritepress.com

Table of Contents

Introduction 1
Chapter 1: The Order of St. Sylvester 4
Chapter 2: Austin & Catherine Mardon.. 9
Chapter 3: Mixing Religion and Psychiatry 14
Chapter 4: The Nomination & Ceremony 20
Chapter 5: Preparing and Travelling to Italy 24
Chapter 6: Roaming in Rome 28
Chapter 7: Beggars: Scam or Real?... 35
Chapter 8: Meeting the Pope 40
Chapter 9: Returning Home 46
Chapter 10: The Pandemic and Changes to Catholic Traditions 50
Conclusion 55

Introduction

The man in white shuffled towards them, grinning. Austin was certain he was about to throw up on the pope's shoes.

A year prior to meeting Pope Francis, Austin and Catherine Mardon had been inducted into the Order of St.Sylvester, an honor they'd never dreamed they'd be receiving. Austin and Catherine had both been diagnosed with a mental illness as young adults and it completely changed the trajectory of their lives. Austin was working on a PhD in geography after completing a NASA mission in Antarctica, when he was diagnosed with schizophrenia. Catherine was working as a successful lawyer in Oklahoma when she was violently attacked, leaving her with Post-Traumatic Stress Disorder and various physical disabilities. They both struggled to accept themselves, as well as find acceptance in their communities. It led them to find each other, resulting in a marriage of over fifteen years, the adoption of a son, and fostering of several other young men with their own mental health challenges. The Mardons became vocal advocates to end the stigma around mental health and other disabilities, but the goal was never to receive recognition, especially not from the pope!

On January 31, 2021 just three months after the Mardons met the pope, Italy confirmed it's first two cases of COVID-19 in Rome. By mid-March, the country had nearly 60 000 cases and the nation was in a complete lockdown. Early on in the pandemic, Italy was one of the hardest hit countries, but many others soon followed suit. The pandemic caused businesses to close and people to be laid off. Travel restrictions led to the separation of families and gathering restrictions meant the cancellation of weddings, birthdays, and other celebrations and traditions. The Catholic Church didn't escape these rules, with masses all over the world being indefinitely suspended. Many traditions such as shaking hands, receiving communion, and kissing the pope's ring, were halted. It's difficult to say in what capacity these practices will resume post-pandemic, if at all. Virtual masses were also introduced during the pandemic and this could cause lasting changes in how people practice their faith.

The pandemic caused isolation and fear, which has likely harmed the mental health of millions. In times of struggles such as these, some people turn to their faith. Unfortunately, Catholicism and psychiatry often haven't had a positive relationship. The two have long misunderstood each other which makes it difficult for Catholics to receive mental health care, as well as for mental health professionals to reach Catholics. Austin and Catherine Mardon both grew up Christian and have experienced mental health challenges, so they understand firsthand the conflict between the two. Although not always treated well by priests and other church members, Austin and Catherine have learned to lean into their faith during their struggles. In order to help bridge the gap between the two, Austin has given talks to priests about the importance of mental health and encouraging their parishioners to seek professional support. Becoming members of the Order of St.Sylvester is another step towards reconciling the strife between the Catholic Church and the field of psychiatry. The Vatican has officially acknowledged the impact of the global pandemic on people's mental health and Pope Francis has begun to talk more openly about it as well. Although a good start, the Mardons believe there is a lot more that needs to be done.

This book details the Mardon's journey from receiving a letter from the Vatican, to their order induction ceremony in Edmonton, to then travelling to Rome and meeting Pope Francis. Along the way they openly discuss issues many are facing both pre and post-pandemic. The conflict between Catholicism and psychiatry is explained and Austin and Catherine share how they think reconciliation could begin. Throughout the book the Mardons reveal the reality of travelling as people who have disabilities in a country that can be largely inaccessible. They talk about the people they saw and how homelessness is visibly an issue in Rome. The book also discusses the effects of COVID-19 on the Catholic Church and their predictions for the future.

It's important to note this book focuses on Catholicism. Other religions may have different beliefs around mental health, vaccines, and the pandemic. Though backed by some scientific research, many of the views expressed in this book are the Mardon's opinions and not reflective of the experience of all Catholics or all people who have a mental illness. The Mardons draw on their personal experience and hope it gives readers insight into what it's like to be inducted into the Order of St.Sylvester and meet the pope.

Chapter 1

The Order of St. Sylvester

The Order of St.Sylvester is one of the five papal orders of knighthood given on behalf of the pope. The title papal, or pontifical, is used because they're the only orders awarded directly by the pope. The orders from highest rank to lowest are as follows:

Supreme Order of Christ
Order of the Golden Spur
Order of Pius IX
Order of St.Gregory the Great
Order of St.Sylvester

The highest two orders are rarely given and tend to be reserved for sovereigns or heads of state. The last time someone was inducted into the Supreme Order of Christ was in 1987, but with the death of King Baudoin of Belgium in 1993, there are no longer any living members. The same goes for the Order of the Golden Spur with the last living member, the Grand Duke Jean of Luxembourg, dying in 2010. It's unknown when, if ever, another member will be inducted into either order. The remaining three orders are more often given to lay people but can include royalty and politicians as well. Although affiliated with the Catholic Church and given by the pope, recipients don't have to be catholic or identify with any religion. The only people exempt from becoming members of any of the orders are priests and other clergy. Although rare, it's possible to be bumped from a lower class to a higher one by the pope after an initial nomination. Becoming a member of any of the orders of knighthood is a lifelong honor, meaning the title can't be stripped.

The Order of St.Sylvester is the lowest of the five papal orders but is actually one of the oldest. The full title is the Pontifical Equestrian Order of St.Sylvester Pope and Martyr, however it was originally called the Order of the Golden Spur. In the 1900's an influx of people began being inducted into the order. Membership was being granted at an unusually rapid rate because rather than receiving approval from the pope, many people simply paid for the award. With more and more people being able to easily buy their way in, it quickly depreciated the value of the order. Hoping to return it to it's former prestige, in 1841 Pope Gregory XVI changed the name of the order to the Order of St.Sylvester and the Golden Militia. He stripped the honor from anyone who'd received it in a way other than a Papal Brief — a formal document given by the pope. Pope Gregory then limited the number of people allowed to be inducted into the order to just 150 commanders and 300 knights. In 1905 Pope Pius X reformed the order again. This time it was separated into two orders, one named the Order of the Golden Spur and the other the Order of St.Sylvester. The membership limit was removed as well. No reformations have been made to the order since.

The order was named after St.Sylvester I because he was one of the original founders. It's likely there were multiple, but it's unknown exactly who they all were. St.Sylvester was pope from the year 314 until he died in 335. Being pope for a total of 21 years, makes him one of the top 10 longest serving popes in history. His feast day is celebrated in the west on December 31st, New Year's Eve, while the eastern feast day is celebrated a few days later on January 2nd. Much of St.Sylvester's life remains a mystery, but many stories have been speculated. Some legends say he was taken in by a priest as a child and his job was to welcome Christian travellers, give them a place to stay, and offer help in any other way he could (Catholic News Agency). Another popular story claims he cured the Roman emperor Constantine of leprosy, then converted and baptized him, making him the first Christian Roman emperor (Editors of Encyclopedia Britannica). Although it's unknown if these stories are fictional, it's true St.Sylvester did a lot for Christianity. Many churches were built while he was pope including the largest catholic church in the world, St.Peter's Basilica. St.Peter's Basilica is supposedly the burial site of St.Peter who was the first pope and an apostle of Jesus. To this day, the pope still holds mass here on special occasions and people travel from all over the world to see it in Rome.

The honor of becoming a member of the Order of St.Sylvester is given to people who are involved in the work of the church or their community through their career or various artistic mediums including music and painting. Nominations can be made by bishops, archbishops, or nuncios. Each nominee's file must be approved by the pope before they're inducted into the order. Originally only men could become members and were given the title of knight, but in 1994 St.John Paul II inducted the first woman into the order and bestowed her the title of dame. There are four classes within the order of St.Sylvester and from highest to lowest they are:

Knight/Dame Grande Cross (1st Class)
Knight/Dame Commander with Star (2nd Class)
Knight/Dame Commander (3rd Class)
Knight/Dame (4th Class)

No specific duties are required of order members, though they may be asked to partake in important events at their diocese such as the consecration of bishops and ordination of priests. There are two remaining historical perks bestowed upon members: the allowance to carry a sword in the presence of the pope and the ability to ride a horse inside any church including St.Peter's Basilica. Although interesting, the latter of these privileges hasn't been taken advantage of in many years.

When invited to participate in ceremonies at their diocese, order members typically wear their uniform. Each of the five papal orders has a unique uniform, but they do share some similarities. All knights carry swords and wear hats, while all dames wear capes and black lace mantillas, and both knights and dames must wear white gloves (Association of Papal Orders in Ireland). Upon being initiated into the Order of St.Sylvester each person receives a golden maltese cross. It's similar to a regular cross, but each arm splits into a 'v'. On one side there's a picture of St.Sylvester and on the other side "1841 Gregorius XVI restituit" is engraved in honor of Pope Gregory and the reformations he made to the order. The medallion is gold and black, and the arms of the cross are white. It's attached to a black and red striped ribbon, to be easily worn. The official St.Sylvester uniform differs depending on which class someone is a member of, as well as their gender. The uniform for all knights is a black coat and buttons with gold details. The higher the class, the more detailing there is. They also wear a bi-cornered hat which the Knight Grande Cross wears a white feather in. Each class has a different version of the maltese cross medallion on their chest or around their neck. The Knight Grande Cross wears a sash across their body which the medal hangs from and a star on the left side of their chest. Knight Commander with a Star wears the same star on their breast but no sash and instead wears the medal around their neck. The Knight

Commander wears the medal around their neck as well, while the Knight wears the medal on the left side of their chest. Dames of every class wear the black lace mantilla, capes, and white gloves. The official uniforms tend to be reserved for special occasions. Members are not actually given the uniform, they have to buy it themselves and the men's uniform is quite expensive which is why many members don't purchase it.

There have been hundreds, possibly thousands, of recipients and because of this it's nearly impossible to have a single list of all of the members in the Order of St.Sylvester. Many private member associations around the world keep their own lists, but they're by no means exhaustive. These associations help fellow knights and dames from any of the five orders connect with each other and lead as examples in their communities. A well known member of the Order of St.Sylvester is Oskar Schindler, a German industrialist who saved hundreds of Jews during the Holocaust. Another famous member is British comedian, actor, and singer, Bob Hope. Many princes, prime ministers, authors, and artists are also members, a group Austin and Catherine Mardon are now officially a part of as well. The Order of St.Sylvester has been around for over one hundred years. Becoming a member is something few people achieve in their lifetime, yet Austin and Catherine earned the honor through their resiliency and selflessness.

References

Association of Papal Orders in Ireland (n.d.). [Webpage]. Retrieved from https://www.papalorders.ie/index.php/pontifical-booklet

Catholic News Agency (n.d.). [Webpage]. Retrieved from https://www.catholicnewsagency.com/saint/st-sylvester-pope-101

Editors of Encyclopedia Britannica. St.Sylvester I (n.d.). [Webpage]. https://www.britannica.com/biography/Saint-Sylvester-I

Wikipedia. Orders, decorations, and medals of the holy see [Webpage]. Retrieved from https://en.wikipedia.org/wiki/Orders,_decorations,_and_medals_of_the_Holy_See

Chapter 2

Austin & Catherine Mardon

Austin and Catherine Mardon were nominated for the Order of St.Sylvester by Father Patrick, the priest who performed their marriage ceremony over 15 years ago. Like most things in the Mardons' lives, their love story wasn't exactly uneventful. They met online, were engaged after meeting once, and married three months after that. From the beginning, their relationship was tested. Catherine moved to Canada to be with Austin, but was threatened with deportation by Austin's family who claimed she was an eco-terrorist and forced her to undergo RCMP and FBI checks. Then, their civil ceremony almost didn't happen because the venue was cancelled by his sister the day before and they were forced to move everything to their hotel. The catholic ceremony was even more memorable with guests being locked out of the church and Father Patrick racing to complete the vows before Austin's family were able to barge in. The Mardons joke Father Patrick nominated them simply because he felt bad for what they'd endured. In actuality he nominated them for the work they've done with the mental health and disabled communities. Some people are skeptical of how a seemingly regular couple from Alberta were inducted into a prestigious papal order, but Austin and Catherine have shown time and again they're deserving of the honor. The Mardons have dedicated their lives to being advocates for people who have a mental illness or other disabilities. They both have their own experiences with mental health challenges and rather than letting it control their lives, they've turned it into a strength and used it to help others who have been through similar things.

Austin was diagnosed with schizophrenia in 1992 when he was 30 years old. At the time, he'd recently returned from a NASA mission in Antarctica and was working towards a PhD in geography. He'd also founded the Antarctic Institute of Canada whose goal was to persuade the Canadian government to invest in further research in Antarctica. Although he'd begun experiencing symptoms of schizophrenia prior to his official diagnosis, he was in denial because he worried it'd cause him to lose his career and educational opportunities. Symptoms he experienced were paranoia, struggling to read body language, erratic and irrational behavior, and hallucinations. When he was a child his mother was diagnosed with schizophrenia which made Austin well aware of what it looked like, yet he refused to see it in himself. Seeing how people treated his mother, Austin feared he'd be treated similarly and again be bullied as he'd been when his classmates discovered his mother's diagnosis. When Austin was diagnosed, the doctors at the hospital told him his life was over, he'd likely never be able to have a career or a family, and his chances of becoming homeless were high. It took a long time for Austin to accept his diagnosis, but once he did, he began to advocate for himself and others like him. Austin completed his PhD in geography and began receiving recognition for his scholarly research articles, as well as for speaking out about schizophrenia. He became a member of the Order of Canada in 2006, an honor given to those who make a significant contribution to the country. He was awarded it for his advocacy work and the contributions he'd made to improve the lives of people living with schizophrenia and other mental illnesses.

Catherine was working as a lawyer in Oklahoma when she became entangled in the investigation of a white supremacist group. After standing trial against them she was attacked by one of the members while leaving her office. Catherine was stabbed 17 times and thrown down a flight of stairs. She sustained serious injuries, including severe nerve damage in her back and legs, leaving her unable to walk for eight years. She also had chronic pain and a traumatic brain injury which caused partial aphasia. Due to this she was unable to continue working. After the attack Catherine also began experiencing symptoms of Post-Traumatic Stress Disorder. These symptoms included avoiding crowds, loud places, and emotionally charged situations. She also experienced nightmares and flashbacks regularly. Similarly to Austin, she too had difficulties accepting what was happening and tried to ignore and hide the symptoms for years. Eventually she was forced to come to terms with her diagnosis and seek help from a psychologist. She too became an advocate and volunteered as a lawyer for those who were homeless or had a mental illness. Years later, Catherine wrote Curveballs, a book which details her life and experiences with a mental illness and physical disability. It's an inspiring book that shows it's possible to move forward even after severe trauma.

In 2012, a few years after Austin and Catherine were married, they began fostering a young boy. The Mardons knew the boy's mom before she passed away and had agreed to take him in when she got sick. She had Bipolar Disorder and had struggled with her mental health and other challenges; it made the boy's childhood difficult. While living with them as a teenager he was diagnosed with Fetal Alcohol Spectrum Disorder. It was a shock for them all, but they continued to try to support him as best they could. When he turned 18 they officially adopted him. He made a few unhealthy choices and put Catherine and Austin in some difficult situations, though they never gave up on him and continued to love him unconditionally. Although his life hasn't been an easy one, having the support of Austin and Catherine has helped. Knowing themselves what it feels like to be cast aside because of a mental illness, Austin and Catherine didn't want others to have to go through what they did. This prompted them to begin fostering other young adults. All of the boys they've had in their care have had some type of psychological disorder, most often FASD like their son. All of the boys were turning 18, meaning they were about to age out of their group or foster homes. The majority of them hadn't been taught the skills they needed to be able to live on their own and they didn't have anywhere to go. The Mardons took them in and acted as caregivers, mentors, and role models to support them in realizing the full life they could live. Father Patrick knew their son and other foster children well and he understood the challenges the Marsons faced in supporting them. The priest saw the personal sacrifices they made and the selfless love they gave, and for this he believed they were worthy of being nominated for the Order of St.Sylvester.

Austin and Catherine's volunteering goes well beyond fostering. They've done a lot of other advocacy work for people who have mental illnesses and disabilities, including giving hundreds of speeches on the topics of schizophrenia, the importance of mental health, and persevering after a diagnosis. Their advocacy work has even gone so far as to help in the development of local government policies. Local electees have often consulted them on programs and policies for homeless youth and mental health. The Mardons strive to be a voice for those who aren't always given a seat at the table. They aren't paid, trying to leverage power, or have a secret agenda. They just have personal experience and the stories of their foster boys. Austin is also an adjunct professor of psychiatry at the University of Alberta and Austin and Catherine are both on various mental health committees and boards.

Austin founded the Antarctic Institute of Canada in 1985. It began with the goal of persuading the Canadian government to allocate more funds to research in Antarctica, but it grew into something else entirely. In the beginning, it consisted only of Austin writing various articles and books about geography. Wishing to expand his reach Austin brought on students to help write. Each student brought their own area of speciality, broadening the scope of topics greatly. Having experienced the challenges of getting into graduate school, Austin and Catherine decided to use AIC as a tool to help young writers, designers, and editors get published and build their portfolios. AIC is now an official non-profit and has published over two hundred books and countless articles, many of which centre around mental health. The book Alphabet Soup, explains various psychological disorders and recounts the real life experiences of people who live with them. Societal Conflict and the Stigma of People with Addiction explores society's position on addiction and how the stigma surrounding it separates people from the support they need. These are only a few examples of the books which attempt to explain mental health and psychological disorders in an easy-to-understand way. Rather than regurgitate clinical terms, they often use information from people who have lived experience with mental illness and disabilities. AIC also developed the beloved Gandy series, inspired by the Mardons real-life mischievous basset hound. Although children's books, they cover a range of important topics including mental health. Through these books and others like them, Austin and Catherine have made research based knowledge more accessible. It also helps to spread awareness about mental health and to lessen the stigma associated with it. The Mardons believe the books are important, but the real product is the students. Seeing their growth and being able to support them on their journey to making a difference in the world makes the stress of running AIC worth it. Many of their students have gone on to medical school, law school, and other masters programs.

Despite Austin and Catherine having been awarded various honors including the Order of St.Sylvester, Austin thinks a lot of people continue to see him as a failure because he hasn't necessarily succeeded in the traditional financial or social sense. Yet both Catherine and Austin feel they've had great successes in other areas of their lives. One such area is their foster boys' and students' growth. To some, it may seem like a small accomplishment but Austin views the smallest changes as making the biggest differences. Austin says instead of people getting stuck on the big issues, everyone needs to start with the small ones. Essentially he and Catherine live by the motto "act locally, impact globally". If people start striving to make small changes like Austin and Catherine, then other people get on board and eventually it builds and builds until it's making a large impact, forcing more people to take notice. Being inducted into the Order of St.Sylvester proves this. Austin and Catherine weren't allowed to see the file about them that was sent to the pope, but Austin thinks they probably said he was crazy, which he jokes he is. The church and the field of psychiatry have had a complicated relationship for centuries but perhaps Austin and Catherine being inducted as members begins to mark a turning point.

Chapter 3

Mixing Religion and Psychiatry

Historically, the Church played a significant role in mental health care. This changed as the field of psychology became more pronounced and Freud's ideas of psychoanalysis were popularized. As the two became more separated, the belief that religion and psychiatry don't mix well, became more common. Science has often had a complex relationship with religion, but it seems psychiatry more so than other fields. Psychiatrists on average are less likely to be religious than any other type of physician (Ayvaci, 2016). Exact reasoning for this is unknown but the disconnect seemingly goes both ways as many religious people struggle with the idea of psychiatry as well. In the past, the Catholic Church saw mental illness as a demonic possession and some still believe it comes from "weakness in faith" and can be cured by "willpower alone" (Ayvaci, 2016). This belief penetrates various levels of the Catholic Church, from parishioners, to priests, to bishops. The danger in these beliefs is it deters people from reaching out for support which can cause suffering, isolation, and even lead to harming oneself or others. However, it's important to note the stigma surrounding mental illness is an issue that spreads far beyond the Catholic Church. If a religious person does seek help for their mental health, typically they go to their clergy first. Unfortunately, studies have shown priests tend to be dismissive of mental health concerns, either due to a lack of interest or limited training in psychology (Ayvaci, 2016; Weaver, 2010). This can dissuade a person from reaching out again because their concerns have been invalidated. Clearly disconnection between the Catholic Church and psychiatry is harmful to parishioners. It's possible however, changes are beginning as people like Catherine and Austin share how their mental health and faith journeys have intertwined.

The Mardons understand the complex relationship between psychiatry and religion better than many because they're both practicing Christians and have also experienced mental health challenges. They believe the Church and psychiatrists need to work more closely together in the interest of helping people. Unfortunately, Austin hasn't always received support from his church community regarding his mental health. Some fellow parishioners don't fully understand schizophrenia. They believe he shouldn't take medication for it because prayer should be enough to heal him. Austin is an advocate for proper medication and credits it for his experience of fewer schizophrenia symptoms. Catherine and Austin believe if someone breaks their leg they go to the doctor and are prescribed medication and having a psychological disorder like schizophrenia is no different. Priests have also treated Austin poorly on occasion. Some have wanted to exorcise him while others cross themselves three times when he speaks. They hold onto the belief that he's possessed rather than having a diagnosed psychological disorder. Catherine hasn't had many of these experiences, perhaps in part because schizophrenia is more closely tied to religion than some other mental illnesses. One study found nearly half of all people who have schizophrenia have religious delusions (Krzystanek, Krysta, Klasik & Krupka-Matuszczyk, 2012, p.68). Austin is one such person. He jokes that everybody talks to God but only those who have schizophrenia say God talks back. In his hallucinations he's seen angels and twinkling lights. To him, these were special, spiritual moments, but others label him as insane. Austin doesn't understand why people have faith in God without seeing proof, but when he sees signs they call him crazy. Because of this, he doesn't often talk about it. However, Austin thinks religious experiences are part of the human experience, regardless of having a mental illness. Historically and contemporarily there have been many "Road to Damascus" experiences recorded. The Road to Damascus is the story of Saul journeying to Damascus when Jesus suddenly appears to him, making him blind. Ananias then gives Saul back his sight. Saul converts to Christianity, is baptized as Paul, and goes forth to spread the word of Jesus. It's now used as a common saying meaning a type of epiphany that causes someone to make a big change. Austin argues this is evidence religious experiences like his hallucinations can happen to anyone, someone with a mental illness or not, a religious follower or not.

Austin believes much of the hesitancy around psychology for priests comes from Freud's legacy. Freud believed religion was an obsessional neurosis and wasn't based on divinity, but rather on the human need for protection and God fulfills the role of parent in adulthood (Palmer, 1997). Clearly, this is in disagreement with many Catholic beliefs. In Catholicism, God is treated as a divinity and can't be explained as simply a coping mechanism of the human brain. Austin himself aligns more closely with the ideas of Carl Jung, Freud's associate. He studied both religion and psychology and how the two interacted for a person to be able to find wholeness (Palmer 1997). Austin believes Jung's theory could help bridge the gap between religion and psychiatry. Educating priests on psychology and mental health, as well as teaching psychiatrists about religion, could be a place to start in Austin's opinion. On a few occasions Austin has been asked by his local bishop to talk to a group of priests about medication and the importance of being on the same team as psychiatrists. Austin doesn't think priests should try to be doctors or that doctors should pretend to be priests, but he does believe they should support each other. It could be simple things like suggesting someone listen to their doctor or take their medication. Austin has met some priests who see taking medication as a character flaw. He explains to them it's actually a sign of strength because taking medication means accepting a diagnosis and dealing with difficult side effects. It takes a lot of bravery, even more so when support from family, church, or society, is lacking. He thinks with more cooperation and understanding people will be more willing to get help, try medication, and stick with it.

Another point of contention between catholics and advocates for mental health was how in the Code of Canon Law, death by suicide meant a person couldn't have a Catholic burial. In 1983 a revision to this law changed that, although death by suicide continues to be stigmatized by many Catholic folk. The bible itself doesn't necessarily condemn suicide but some people still see it as a sin. Death by suicide is argued to fall under the the fifth commandment "though shalt not kill". This can cause even more hurt for family and friends who have a loved one die this way. Many religious people however do acknowledge death by suicide is most often due to a mental illness, which the person cannot always control. The Vatican has made it clear they do not condone euthanasia or assisted suicide. They've gone so far as to say those choosing to end their lives cannot receive the sacraments. This is a difficult situation for people with chronic illnesses, which in some countries includes mental illness, and their families. These topics are controversial in many other religions, but also among people who aren't religious. It's a divisive topic even within the mental health field.

The Mardons believe in reaching struggling people where they're at. This could mean mental health agencies partnering with religious communities in order to support people in accessing the help they need. Strengthening the relationship between religion and mental health could be beneficial to many. Studies have shown psychiatric patients often use religion and prayer to cope and it's proven to lessen depression, suicide, anxiety, and substance abuse (Koenig, 2009; Weber & Pargament, 2014). "Positive religious coping methods (e.g. spiritual support, positive religious reframing of stressors, and spiritual connectedness) are significantly associated with and predictive of better mental health and psychological well being generally" (Weber & Pargament, 2014). Austin himself has found a lot of comfort in his faith when he's struggled with his mental health. If the church community and field of psychiatry can reconcile, it's possible more people could feel supported in this way, rather than having the two worlds be separate. Easily accessible clergy and other religious resources could be introduced in hospitals where people are struggling with mental health. People with a mental health challenge have shown to benefit from a supportive religious community (Weber & Pargament, 2014). Essentially, if it's proven to be helpful, even in a small amount, it should be an available option for patients.

Pope Francis has also begun to speak out about the importance of mental health, especially during the COVID-19 pandemic. In a 2019 interview he talked about his own experience of seeing a psychologist to help with his anxiety. Francis shared he saw a psychiatrist weekly for six months when he lived in Argentina because of the stress he experienced while helping refugees escape the volatile government (Mares, 2021). During the interview, the pope said his psychiatrist taught him how to manage his anxiety, in particular while making difficult decisions, and he believes her teachings continue to be useful to him even now (Mares, 2021). One technique he uses to calm his anxiety is listening to Bach (Hattrup, 2021). He also shared his belief that all priests should have a basic knowledge of psychology and that there should be a greater collaboration between mental health agencies and religious groups (Mares, 2021; Weaver 2010). Since sharing this, the pope has spoken out a few more times about the significance of mental health. In June 2021 Pope Francis commended the National Conference for Mental Health on the work they were doing and spoke about the importance of strengthening the healthcare system and scientific research in regards to mental health (Hattrup, 2021). Although Pope Francis is one of the first popes to speak so openly about this issue, limited action has been taken by either side towards the goal of collaboration.

The COVID-19 pandemic has taken a serious toll on the mental health of all people and the Church has recognized this in their parishioners.

In 2021 the Vatican released a document titled Accompanying People in Psychological Distress in the Context of the COVID-19 Pandemic: Members of One Body, Loved by One Love. It discusses issues exacerbated by the pandemic including anxiety, depression, and suicidal thought, while encouraging people to join together as a community through social responsibility and solidarity. It encourages people to care for one another, especially the groups most severely affected by the pandemic such as the elderly and homeless. Acknowledging the impact the pandemic has had on mental health is a step in the right direction for the reconciliation of the Catholic Church and psychiatry. Austin and Catherine believe rather than seeing one as superior to the other, the two can complement each other. They're both ways of explaining the world, though sometimes they're contradictory, in the end they hopefully want the same thing — to do no harm. Both have done harm in the past, but perhaps they're equally at fault and shouldn't blame each other. There is still more that can be done by both sides to bridge the gap on individual and institutional levels.

References

Ayvaci, E.M. (2016). Religious barriers to mental health care. The American Journal of Psychiatry, 11(7), 11-13. doi: 10.1176/appi.ajp-rj.2016.110706

Hattrup, K.N. (2021). Pope Francis' tricks for warding off anxiety. Aleteia. Retrieved from https://aleteia.org/2021/06/28/pope-calls-for-overcoming-stigma-of-mental-illness/

Koenig, H.G. (2009). Research on religion, spirituality, and mental health: a review. The Canadian Journal of Psychiatry, 54(5), 283-291. doi: 10.1177/070674370905400502

Krzystanek, M., Krysta, K., Klasik, A., & Krupka-Matuszczyk, I. (2012). Religious content of hallucinations in paranoid schizophrenia. Psychiatria Danubina, 24, 65-69. Retrieved from http://www.psychiatria-danubina.com

Mares, C. (2021). Pope Francis says seeing a psychiatrist helped him with anxiety when he was younger. Catholic News Agency. Retrieved from pope-francis-says-seeing-a-psychiatrist-helped-him-with-anxiety-when-he-was-younger

Palmer, M. (1997). Freud and Jung on Religion. London & New York: Routledge.

Weaver, A. (2010). Through a glass darkly: How Catholics struggle with mental illness. US Catholic, 75(2), 12-17. Retrieved from https://uscatholic.org/articles/201001/through-a-glass-darkly-how-catholics-struggle-with-mental-illness

Weber, S.R., & Pargament, K.I. (2014). The role of religion and spirituality in mental health. Current Opinion in Psychiatry, 27(5), 358-363. doi: 10.1097/YCO.0000000000000080

Chapter 4

The Nomination & Ceremony

The Mardons were picking up groceries for the boys, organizing students, and hosting parties, blissfully unaware of the fact a detailed file of their lives was sitting on the pope's desk. After Father Patrick nominated them for the Order of St.Sylvester, their file was sent to the archbishop, then to the papal nacio, the secretary of state for the vatican, and finally the pope himself. They'd been nominated by Father Patrick for the bottom class, Knight and Dame. Upon seeing their file Pope Francis bumped them to the next highest class, giving them the titles of Knight and Dame Commander. In 2018 Austin and Catherine received an article in the mail from Bishop Greg Bittman about their book, Gandy and the Man in White, which tells the story of Gandy meeting the pope. When they asked him about it he told them they may be receiving more mail in a few days but wouldn't give specifics. Two days later a letter sealed with the pope's wax emblem arrived with "Vatican City" as the return address. A day that had begun so ordinarily, quickly turned into one of the biggest days of their lives. Receiving the letter was a surreal experience. Austin says he was "flabbergasted", he just couldn't believe it. He rushed to show Catherine and for a brief moment she was speechless, until she cried out in dismay and snapped into panic mode. She feared there'd be a huge ceremony where she'd be forced to stand in front of hundreds of people. Catherine has always been shy, but she's also uncomfortable in large groups because of her PTSD. Loud noises like applause can cause her to panic and being surrounded by strong emotions, even positive ones, can be triggers for her. Austin is the complete opposite. He enjoys the spotlight and is happiest being surrounded by people. Knowing this, Catherine told Austin, "You can have a ceremony, but I won't be there". Wanting to respect Catherine's wishes, but also wanting to share this once in a lifetime opportunity with her, he was torn. Eventually he was able to convince Catherine to attend the ceremony after they and the archbishop agreed it would be a small and intimate affair. Rather than the hundreds of people who would traditionally attend, it would just be Austin and Catherine, some of their foster boys, the archbishop, and a couple of the staff from the chapel centre.

The first person the Mardons told about the award was one of their foster sons. Having lived with them for many years he'd seen Austin and Catherine receive a number of awards so initially he didn't quite understand the importance of it. After explaining more about the order and who Pope Francis was, he was very impressed and proud. Next, they told their adopted son. He too was happy for them, but wasn't comfortable attending the ceremony. Shortly after, they began telling friends and family. In the beginning, many people didn't believe them. After all, receiving an award from the pope isn't exactly an everyday occurrence. Austin and Catherine assured them it was true and had the letter from the pope to prove it. A few friends who weren't involved in the Catholic Church didn't know what the Order of St.Sylvester was. When the Mardons explained it, some downplayed the honor, saying "it's just the pope, not a saint or anything". Jealousy can certainly be a great motivator for undermining others' achievements. The Order of St.Sylvester, however, is arguably comparable to the Order of Canada. Having received both, Austin thinks the Order of St.Sylvester could be seen as even more prestigious because it's an international award rather than a national one. The Order of St.Sylvester can be legally recognized in Canada if it's been signed off by the Governor General, the Canadian representative for the Queen. Essentially, if Catherine or Austin were in the military they could be allowed to wear the medal on their uniform, same as the Order of Canada. Although becoming members was a great honor for them, they purposefully chose not to tell Austin's family because they knew it'd upset them. In the past whenever Austin has been in the media for advocacy or awards his family was angry because they believed it highlighted his schizophrenia and they didn't want their name to be tied to that. As Austin predicted, when they eventually did find out about the award, they were quite upset and offered no congratulations. Catherine's family on the other hand were happy and excited for them. Even though some people didn't fully acknowledge the honor of being inducted into the Order of St.Sylvester, Austin and Catherine felt truly blessed to be given such an award.

Catherine and Austin were, as far as they know, the first people in Alberta to receive the honor. There was another member named in Ontario, but because there's no list of members they were unsure if there were any in other parts of Canada. Being the only members in the area they didn't know what the ceremony was supposed to be like. According to Catherine, some larger archdioceses like Toronto and London, have grandiose ceremonies exactly like the opening scene of the Godfather 3. In the movie, they call it the Order of St.Sebastian, but many catholics have claimed it's meant to be the Order of St.Sylvester. The character Michael receives the award for his supposed charitable works. The medal given to him is nearly identical to the Order of St.Sylvester, a maltese cross on a red and black ribbon. Michael also wears a black jacket with gold buttons, white gloves, and a sword, the same uniform as the order. In the movie the archbishop says a prayer and presents the medal to him, then he's required to make vows to the order, followed by a blessing from the archbishop. The enormous church is shown to be filled with people and a large choir can be heard. An extravagant party follows the ceremony.

In reality, Austin and Catherine's ceremony took place at the chapel in the pastoral and administration office of the Archdiocese of Edmonton. It's a humble brick building only able to fit about 40 people. Beautiful stained glass windows cover the back wall and polished wooden pews line the room. At the front is a small dais with an altar and a large crucifix hangs behind it. The archbishop and priest stood at the front with Austin and Catherine while a few friends, family, and some staff from the diocese watched from the pews. A couple of their foster sons attended as well. The Mardons could've chosen to have the ceremony at a larger church like St.Joseph's Basilica, which can seat nearly 1200 people. The ceremony would've been much more extravagant, but knowing the Mardons the archbishop thought they'd appreciate something more intimate and modest, especially Catherine. The Mardons weren't required to say vows like in the movie but they did receive a similar medal to the one Michael got. The archbishop performed a short ceremony and in keeping with the modest theme, there was no extravagant party held afterwards. The Mardons instead had a small get together with a few friends later in the day at their house. Much to Catherine's chagrin, the ceremony was broadcasted on itv for people who weren't able to attend in person. They were also both interviewed for articles in the Lethbridge Newspaper, Austin's alma mater, and the Grandin Newspaper, an Alberta based Catholic media source.

Austin and Catherine received a letter and a signed latin scroll from the pope on December 31st 2018, St.Sylvester's feast day. They've kept them as mementos of one of the most memorable moments of their lives. The Mardons have yet to participate in a ceremony at the church, but haven't had much opportunity due to covid. Austin hopes they'll be asked in the future, though Catherine still dreads having to be in front of a crowd. As Knight and Dame Commander, they now have the ability to wear a sword in the presence of the pope and ride a horse inside any church including St.Peter's Basilica. However, they didn't take advantage of this while in Rome. Whenever Austin sees the archbishop he jokes he just needs to find a horse, preferably a large sturdy one like a clydesdale. The archbishop still isn't completely sure he's only joking.

The ceremony took place just over one year before the Mardons went to Rome to meet the pope. Meeting the pope is not necessary for members inducted into the order, but it was something Catherine and Austin wanted to do. Most order members have a ceremony at their archdiocese but Catherine and Austin decided to take it one step further by going to Rome to meet Pope Francis.

Chapter 5

Preparing and Travelling to Italy

In passing, Catherine casually mentioned she'd love to meet the pope one day. Austin jumped at the opportunity to make her wish come true and potentially embarrass her. In their nearly 15 years of marriage, they'd never been on a trip together. Not even a honeymoon. After their wedding they were struggling financially and dealing with family issues, so a honeymoon wasn't a priority. As anyone with kids will tell you, they quickly became busy with their son and foster kids, leaving no time for a trip. The Mardons decided this trip needed to be a priority. Austin spoke to the archbishop to see if meeting the pope would be feasible and together they spoke to the papal nuncio. In order to meet Pope Francis, Austin and Catherine had to send a request to the Vatican secretary of state. The secretary of state is a cardinal appointed by the pope to handle various diplomatic tasks. Before they knew it, they were approved to fly to Rome to meet Pope Francis! Once they decided beyond a doubt they'd be going, a date needed to be chosen. Catherine suggested they wait a few months, maybe go in March of the next year, but Austin was impatient. He felt they needed to go as soon as possible, so they chose November of 2019. Whether a psychic feeling or a sign from God, they were lucky they did. If they'd waited much longer they likely wouldn't have been able to go because of the COVID-19 pandemic. Austin believes when a wave comes you need to ride it because you can't just get back on. In other words, when an opportunity like meeting the pope presents itself, take it. Austin believes it's part of living life to the fullest and he passes this advice onto his AIC students as well. It was this mindset that made it possible for them to travel to meet the pope.

As flight, accommodation, and other details were discussed by the Mardons and their travel agent, reality of the momentous event began to set in. Ever the giving type, the Mardons began to think about what they'd bring back as souvenirs for their friends and family. Catherine's always been quite crafty and decided to make dozens of rosaries to be blessed by the pope and given as gifts. Using various beads and metal she spent hours making beautiful rosaries of all different colors. The bag ended up being surprisingly heavy and took up a large portion of her suitcase, but Catherine was determined to have them blessed. Catherine's brother requested a St.Christopher's medal blessed by the pope. He'd carried around the same one since he was a boy, but it was beginning to wear out. St.Christopher medals typically portray a man with a child on his back crossing a river. Him crossing the river is a symbol of resiliency and being a helper by supporting others in crossing as well. St.Christopher is also the patron saint of travellers and because most people on any given day have to travel outside their home to some extent, many wear his medallion as a blessing to arrive safely at each destination. It was a fitting symbol for the Mardons as they prepared to travel halfway across the world, but also as advocates and foster parents who helped support others to reach their fullest potential. Inspired by this, while there they brought St.Christopher's medals to be blessed for their foster boys as well.

There was still room in their suitcases but, rather than fill them with essentials like clothing, they chose to fill them with books. Having written and published hundreds of books through AIC, Austin and Catherine wanted to share some of these with the pope. It was difficult to choose only a few but together they agreed upon Curveballs, Screwballs, Gandy and the Man in White, and Gandy and the Lady. Curveballs and Screwballs were written by Catherine. These books tell her story, including the attack which caused her PTSD and physical disabilities, but also the resilience she showed in overcoming it. In the book Catherine also talks about meeting Austin and some of their foster boys. It's an inspiring story and the Mardons thought it would give Pope Francis more insight into who they are. A few books have also been written on Austin's life and his multitude of achievements, as well as his struggle to come to terms with having schizophrenia and his experience since being diagnosed. They didn't want to overwhelm the pope with too many books though, so chose not to include any of them. Austin joked he thought Catherine's story was more interesting anyways. They also brought Gandy and the Man in White both in English and translated into Cree. The book has been translated into various other languages as well, but they thought Pope Francis would be intrigued by the Cree language and it'd maybe spark his interest in visiting Alberta. The Cree people are an Indigenous people in North America and are the largest group of First Nations people in Canada.

Catherine wrote the book because she was intrigued by the idea of what the pope would do if he met a miscreant ragamuffin basset hound like Gandy. It centers around an American professor of geography who travels to Rome to map the catacombs. He brings with him Gandy his service dog, who helps with his PTSD. The professor is taking a break in a park when a priest comes by to give food to the poor and ends up playing fetch with Gandy. The next day the professor and Gandy attend a St.Francis event at St.Peter's Square. The professor then recognizes the man from the other night as the pope. The pope is holding a rosary and Gandy thinks it's a toy. He grabs it from his hand and runs away. The Swiss guards catch Gandy and throw him in a prison. Eventually news of the poor puppy prisoner gets out and people begin calling for his release and sending money to pay for it. The pope releases him, impressed by the amount of people who stepped forward to help a dog. In the end, Gandy and the pope end up walking through the Vatican gardens together as friends. Gandy and the Lady is about Gandy's adventures in Poland and a famous Polish icon, the Black Madonna Czestochowa. It's a painting of the Virgin Mary and there are various legends about her appearing through it. Austin originally wrote it for his Polish friend, but they thought Pope Francis would like it because it focuses on Mary. Thankfully all of the books were quite small so it left enough room for Catherine to also bring yoyos and kites, which she intended to use in St.Peter's Square.

With the pope being the most important living figure in the Catholic Church, not just anyone is invited to meet him, however being a part of the order the Mardons were somewhat pre-vetted. They did have to complete a couple of brief security checks. Being an international body, the pope's security has their own internal background checks rather than regular police checks. It's largely to do with who you know in the church community and because the Mardons knew the archbishop well, he was able to act as a reference for them. Austin had actually undergone the entire process before because he'd met the previous pope, St.John Paul II, in 1996. After completing his NASA mission in Antarctica to recover meteorites, Austin went to Rome to give the pope the papal flag he'd taken with him. Faith has always been important in all aspects of Austin's life, hence why he took the flag to Antarctica. Having met a pope once before, it'd be reasonable to think Austin would be less nervous to meet Pope Francis, but that wasn't the case. His experience with St.John Paul II had been exciting, but Austin will always remember the way the pope seemed to scowl at him. He felt as though St.John Paul II was so godly he could see his sins. It made Austin paranoid Pope Francis would react similarly. Catherine's own nerves about meeting the pope only added to this.

As the date got closer their nerves were amplified. Every small detail seemed to become more important because the pope was involved. At one point Catherine wanted to postpone the trip until April because she didn't think she was thin enough. Deciding what to wear to meet him was difficult, especially because she wasn't completely confident in her body. There'd be reporters and photographers present and this terrified her. Catherine decided on a simple outfit to meet the pope. She wore a green jacket with a black lace manilla, the common uniform for dames, covering her hair. Austin was much less concerned about what to wear, but decided on a black jacket, blue shirt, and blue and red tie. There's no dress code for meeting the pope, though most churches in Rome require women to be covering their shoulders and sometimes their legs as a show of modesty.

Finally the fateful day arrived and they headed to the airport, their luggage weighed down with books and rosaries. They went through regular security at the airport and flew to Toronto and then Rome. The flight was nearly as stressful as the thought of meeting Pope Francis. Catherine wasn't sure she could handle the long flight because of her PTSD. In the 90's when she was working and living in the states she'd been on a plane that malfunctioned. It rapidly descended from 20 000 feet to 5 000 feet in one minute. Nearly a freefall. Catherine hadn't been on a plane since. The first time she went to meet Austin in Edmonton, she chose to take a five day bus ride rather than hop on a plane. Austin and Catherine's mental health challenges affect them every day and that didn't change just because they were on a holiday. Catherine's PTSD and physical disabilities, along with Austin's schizophrenia, affected their choices of what to do and where to go on their trip. They leaned on each other for support and Catherine was able to make it through the flight without having a panic attack.

Chapter 6

Roaming in Rome

The Mardons were quickly distracted from their anxiety when they were surrounded by breathtaking architecture, beautiful holy sites, and the most intriguing people. They'd hired a tour guide to show them around the whole week they were in Rome. Having grown up in Italy she was able to translate for them, but also was able to give them the perspective of a local. Being a licensed tour guide in Italy is a prestigious career, usually requiring a degree. Many even have more than one, or a masters degree. They're also required to pass an in depth exam on the subject they'll be specializing in. Their guide had a major in history and archaeology. She was knowledgeable about the history of each site they visited as well as the Italian customs and people. She was friendly and spunky and they agreed their experience wouldn't have been the same without her. The guide was able to get them special passes into places like the Vatican, saving them from having to wait in line. She also had intimate knowledge of the city and took them to squares they'd never even heard of. Although Austin had been to Rome once before, he was amazed by all of the places he'd yet to see.

When the Mardons first arrived at the airport in Rome they rented a small car to take them to their hotel, but unfortunately Catherine's walker didn't fit in the trunk. While Catherine was attempting to take it apart, the driver was yelling at them in Italian. They were confused and exasperated. Both were exhausted from the long flight and uncomfortably hot from the heat. Although it wasn't unseasonably warm for Rome, it was scorching for two Canadians. Rome definitely didn't make the best first impression on them. Eventually they were able to get a van instead and finally made it to their hotel. The hotel was about 20 feet from St.Peter's Square, in the restricted area, past the soldiers with machine guns. Even in their weary state they were astounded by the beauty and sheer size of St. Peter's Basilica. Jetlagged, they spent the majority of their first day in close proximity to the hotel.

A typical day in Rome for the Mardons started by waking up early and heading to the breakfast buffet at their hotel. Then they'd usually head out for a walk, choosing a new direction each day to explore. On a couple of the days their tour guide picked them up and drove them around to visit different sights. Their trick was to go to the most touristy places before 10am because at that time they were a lot less crowded which Catherine definitely appreciated and Austin enjoyed as well. The majority of their week was spent in St. Peter's Square because they were completely awe struck by it, the people, the structures, the Swiss Guards, everything. They could spend hours people watching, seeing how the tourists and local beggars interacted. The Pontifical Swiss Guard are the military of the Vatican City and bodyguards to the pope. They wear an orange, blue, and red renaissance style uniform and carry a halberd which is similar to a spear, along with more modern weapons. Though shorter than Austin remembers them being, they still looked mean. They were very serious and didn't often smile. There was always something new to see in the square; it was a never ending display of life.

Although happy to stay near the square, the Mardons were somewhat limited in where they could go because of Catherine's disability. Due to spinal damage from her attack, Catherine was unable to walk for eight years. She's since regained much of her mobility, but continues to experience chronic pain. Some days she doesn't notice it much, but other days it's debilitating and feels as though someone is stabbing her in the leg. It's difficult to know which days will be worse, but oftentimes it's triggered by too much movement the previous day. Because of this, Austin was worried Catherine would over-exert herself with all of the walking in Rome. They needed to be wary of how far they went each day and had to hire a van for longer distances. The van was more expensive, but necessary, because as they'd found out on the first day, dismantling Catherine's wheelchair every time was a pain. Even when they were able to take the van, they were still limited because many streets were too small or didn't allow cars. Catherine also re-injured her knee a few years prior to their trip which further limited her mobility. She still has difficulty putting on socks and shoes, walking up stairs, and getting into cars on the passenger side. Catherine uses a walker and after two weeks on the cobblestone streets it was about to break down. Many places in Italy, especially sites outside like the Spanish Steps, were inaccessible to the Mardons because they didn't have a ramp or elevator. Even though they stayed right next to St.Peter's Basilica, they never actually were able to go inside. Every day the line reached across the square and they would've had to wait for hours to get in. Due to Catherine's pain this just wasn't possible. If they go to Rome again they'd like to get a special pass to get them in more quickly. While in Rome Austin and Catherine hardly saw anyone with a walker or wheelchair. They saw a couple of people at the general audience with them and one at a coffee shop, but other than that they didn't see anyone with a visible mobility disability. Italy has one of the oldest populations in the world, second only to Japan. The Mardons wondered if they all just stayed inside because they must have difficulty moving around the city. Afterall, they'd only been there a week and it'd been a challenge. The cobblestones and other architectural features of Rome were largely built when accessibility wasn't considered. In June 2019 the mayor of Rome announced they'd be removing the cobblestone from many of the main streets and transferring it to the smaller walking streets instead. This does help the issue, but still doesn't make it completely accessible for people with wheelchairs or walkers. Despite the inaccessibility of Rome, Austin and Catherine still appreciated the parts they were able to see. They were proud of how well they got to know St.Peter's Square and the people within it. It made them feel almost like locals.

While in Rome, their guide took them to explore various famous landmarks including the Coliseum, the Aurelian Walls, and the Trevi fountain. They were astounded by the sheer size of the Coliseum but Austin's favorite was the Trevi Fountain. They enjoyed it so much they visited twice, once in the morning and again in the evening. Traditionally a person is supposed to throw a coin with their right hand over their left shoulder. The myth says if you toss one coin you'll return to Rome, two coins means a new romance, and three coins leads to marriage. Both Austin and Catherine threw one coin, in hopes of returning to Rome. They also had the opportunity to explore the Vatican museum. The Vatican museum is inside the Vatican City walls and contains the Sistine Chapel, where two of Michelangelo's most famous works are — his ceiling frescoes and the Last Judgement. Because of Catherine's limited mobility in her legs, stairs can be difficult so she needed to take the elevator in the Sistine Chapel. While on it, the elevator came to a grinding halt about halfway up and wouldn't move. She was stuck. Suddenly nearly 30 guards converged on her, all screaming at her in Italian. She had no idea what they were saying. Their tour guide began yelling back at them in Italian as hundreds of people stopped to stare at the commotion. Catherine was mortified. Austin found it hilarious. He joked maybe she'd just saved the pope from being stuck on a broken elevator. Eventually they were able to get the elevator moving and Catherine was alright, more embarrassed than she'd ever been, but alright. Other than this small hiccup, the Mardons thought the Sistine Chapel was breathtaking. Austin thinks catholic churches are so magnificent because Catholics like beautiful things. Although Austin had been to Rome once before, everything was even more magnificent than he remembered. As anyone will tell you, photos and memories simply don't do justice to the real thing. Austin also wanted to take Catherine to the famous La Bocca della Verita - The Mouth of Truth. It's a Roman sculpture in the shape of a man's head with an open mouth and it's famously in a scene from the movie Roman Holiday. Legend says if a liar places their hand inside the mouth, it'll be bitten off. Unfortunately they weren't able to make it there on this trip but, Austin and Catherine would definitely like to go back to explore more of Rome and other parts of Italy.

In addition to it's historical sites, Italy of course is also well known for it's cuisine. Austin's favorites were the limoncello and coffee. Catherine's favorite was any pizza because she believes you can never go wrong with pizza in Rome! They ate copious amounts of pizza and sandwiches. Restaurants were quite expensive but they were able to enjoy a lot of the smaller vendors and coffee shops. One of their favorite places actually wasn't even run by Italians. It was a little pizzeria run by an Iraqi man. Austin and Catherine ordered lunch and dinner for take out one day and his whole face lit up because of the large order. Austin says it was the best spaghetti they ate the whole time they were there.

Catherine was absolutely blown away by St.Peter's Square and Basilica. She was in disbelief of the beauty of it all. She was determined to fly a kite in St.Peter's Square because she thought it'd be a beautiful place to do something she enjoys. Unfortunately, because the square is surrounded by many buildings and a circle of pillars, they essentially block the wind, making it impossible to fly a kite. Luckily Catherine brought her back up hobby, disc golf. She used the garbage cans that dot the square as though they were the chained baskets used for disc golf. Although she received some quizzical looks, she enjoyed herself immensely. It's a reminder to do the things you love, regardless of what other people might think. Going into the trip they knew being a part of the Order of St.Sylvester was special but they didn't realize how important it was. With all the time they spent near the square they truly appreciated not having to be searched when entering or exiting. Normally people and their bags are searched but the guards yelled out "Silvestro!" to each other when the Mardons walked by. They wore their lapel pins, which are much smaller and more modest than the full sized medals, in order to be recognizable.

Austin travelled outside of Rome only once during their week there. A psychiatrist from the middle east who Austin knew, happened to be there at the same time and requested he come speak to a small group of other professionals. Austin went, while Catherine enjoyed a day of roaming the square by herself. He spoke to the group about the importance of mental health and his own experience of having schizophrenia. Even in another country and on vacation Austin was being an advocate for mental health!

St.Peter's Square and Basilica, just steps away from the Mardon's hotel.

Austin in front of St.Peter's Basilica at night.

Austin's favorite spot in Rome, the Trevi Fountain.

Two Swiss Guards standing watch in front of St.Peter's Basilica.

Chapter 7

The Truth Behind Beggars

The extravagant and expensive churches and buildings in Rome were juxtaposed by the poverty stricken people sitting outside. Beggars and homeless people are a common sight in big cities, especially ones as touristy as Rome. Begging was legalized in Italy in the 1990's, meaning supposedly beggars can no longer be persecuted or fined. However, some towns in Italy have gotten around this law by making it illegal to give money to beggars. It's believed this will discourage beggars from congregating in central parts of the city. Other cities have completely disregarded the law and have begun giving fines to people who are seen begging. There's a lot of conflict about whether these rules are doing more help or harm. It's possible it discourages fake beggars while encouraging real homeless people to seek help from shelters and other agencies, but it could also serve to isolate these people further. Fake begging has become somewhat of an industry in Italy. Professional beggars are people who aren't actually homeless but choose to beg to make a living. Some researchers believe begging has a large cultural influence and is considered respectable or at least accepted by certain groups or at certain times. (Delap, 2009; Thommasen, 2019). It's estimated to be quite a lucrative business with unsuspecting tourists as their main targets. The Mardons saw a lot of this, particularly in St.Peter's Square. One woman they saw looked like she had a broken leg, but upon closer examination, they realized it was a makeshift cast made of bubble wrap. Another woman wore tattered clothes but, Catherine pointed out to Austin the woman's shoes were more expensive than his. The woman must've overheard because the next day when they passed her she wasn't wearing shoes. This time Catherine commented that the woman had an expensive looking pedicure. The following day the woman was back again, but this time wearing socks riddled with holes. She wouldn't go near the Mardons though. They also saw a few beggars leave in expensive cars when their "shift" was done.

As Austin and Catherine spent more time in the square, they began to notice patterns. The square was practically empty each morning and evening, but during the day it became overrun with tourists. There were hordes and hordes of people. Each tour guide had a flag with a country on it to symbolize the language they spoke. There was Italian, German, English and dozens of other languages. Tourists would find a guide who spoke their language and pay to do the tour of St.Peter's Basilica with them. Professional beggars purposefully targeted the people on these tours because they knew they were tourists. Locals tended to be more aware of the scammers and refused them money, but many tourists were unaware, making them easier targets. When Austin and Catherine first arrived they were hounded by many of the beggars. As people began to recognize them and realized they wouldn't give money, they were left alone. Catherine had brought a gigantic bag of Canadian pennies with her on the trip because Canada no longer used them. They were intended for throwing in the fountains, but she had some left over on their last day. She decided to give them to one of the women who they'd repeatedly seen begging and carrying around her child throughout the week. Catherine dropped the pennies in front of the women, but wasn't particularly paying attention. As another woman came running and screaming at Catherine she realized she'd given the coins to the wrong woman. They were extremely territorial about their spots and were often quite aggressive. More than once, Austin and Catherine had to yell "no!" at beggars who wouldn't leave them alone. Some scammers are even less passive, they force a service or product on someone and then make them pay for it. Not everyone considers this a form of begging because there's an exchange of goods, even though they may not be wanted (Andriotis, 2016). For example, one man insisted the Mardons take a small plastic elephant from him. He returned later saying they hadn't paid for it. They tried to return the small object because they didn't actually want it, but the man wouldn't take it so they were forced to give him money. They learned after this instance not to accept any "gifts".

In order to gain sympathy from tourists, professional beggars use a variety of tactics. Some women carry around babies or young children. The children look old enough to be able to walk on their own but they look too sickly to be able to do so. Austin and Catherine's tour guide told them that these women actually drug the children so they look sick and don't move. This way they can carry them around all day to receive more sympathy and earn extra money. Similarly, children old enough to beg on their own are used because people tend to give them more money. This has led to an increase in child trafficking for the purpose of begging. Children are often kidnapped by strangers, but also sometimes by people they know such as relatives or their own parents because it can be a lucrative business, making upwards of 15 euros a day per child (Cherneva, 2011). The children are not treated well, even if it's their own family. They may be drugged, starved, or mutilated to receive more sympathy and bring in more money (Cherneva, 2011). If they don't make a certain amount of money each day they're often beaten (Cherneva, 2011; Delap, 2009). There's evidence that informing tourists about the truth behind begging children and telling them not to give money, essentially cutting off the money supply to the traffickers, would help decrease child trafficking (Cherneva, 2011). Many people don't feel comfortable not giving something. Researchers suggest giving children food is a better option to help them (Cherneva, 2011). People also beg with dogs to gain more sympathy. In Italy it's currently illegal to beg using children or animals, but this law is often broken. Some beggars also purposely use religion, either through the location of begging near a church door, or symbols such as crosses or images of the Virgin Mary (Thomassen, 2015). It's possible this is to play towards the idea that giving is necessary for a faithful religious person, not just in Catholicism but other religions as well (Andriotis, 2016). The Mardons noticed the majority of beggars they saw were indeed around St.Peter's Square.

It's important to remember homelessness and poverty are serious issues in Rome and not all beggars are scammers. In 2014 Rome had the second highest homeless population in Italy at 7709 people (Feantsa, 2017). These people don't beg for the day to scam tourists, but rather because it's a means to survive. Many times their situation is caused by factors they can't necessarily control. Homelessness is often due to unemployment, family issues, and difficulties immigrating (Braga & Corno, 2011). Another major contributor to homelessness and poverty is mental health. Psychotic illnesses, drug and alcohol addictions, and major depression are all more prevalent in homeless populations than in the rest of the community (Fazel, Khosla, Doll, & Geddes, 2008). Austin takes this issue to heart because when he was diagnosed with schizophrenia, he was told he'd likely be homeless. The Mardons have also been involved with helping homeless youth in their home city, especially those with mental health challenges.

Pope Francis has always been vocal about the need for people to help the homeless. As the first of his name, he chose it in honor of St.Francis of Assisi. St.Francis famously helped the poor. He gave away all of his wealth and possessions and lived among them, following and preaching the word of God, and founding the Franciscan Orders. He's one of the patron saints of Italy as well. Pope Francis has lived by simpler means than other popes and has placed an emphasis on supporting the poor. Austin finds it intriguing he was able to meet the first pope named after St.Francis, because his dad actually prayed to St.Francis before Austin was born in hopes he'd receive a son. His father said he would dedicate his son to St.Francis if it happened. When Austin was young, his father often talked about St.Francis and all of the amazing things he did. It's fitting the Mardons were able to meet a pope who cares so much for homeless people as it's an issue they've been focused on for a long time as well.

References

Andriotis, K. (2016). Beggars - tourists' interactions: an unobtrusive typological approach. Tourism Management, 52, 64-73. doi: j.tourman.2015.06.006

Braga, M. & Corno L. (2011). Being homeless: Evidence from Italy. Giornale degli Economisti e Annali di Economia, 70(Anno 124)(3), 33-73. http://www.jstor.org/stable/41756379.

Cherneva, I. (2011). Human trafficking for begging. Buffalo Human Rights Law Review, 25, 26-73. Retrieved from: https://digitalcommons.law.buffalo.edu/bhrlr/vol17/iss1/2

Delap, E. (2009). Begging for change: Research findings and recommendations on forced child begging in Albania/Greece, India, and Senegal. Anti-Slavery International, 1-33. doi: 978-0-900918-73-5

Fazel, S., Khosla, V., Doll, H., & Geddes, J. (2008). The prevalence of mental disorders among the homeless in western countries: Systematic review and meta-regression analysis. PLoS Medicine, 5(12), 1670-1681. doi: 10.1371/journal.pmed. 0050225

Feantsa. (2017). [pdf] Retrieved from https://www.feantsa.org/download/it-proof-read-new-template124857004325179404.pdf

Thomassen, B. (2015). Begging Rome: Norms at the margins, norms of the in-between. Critique of Anthropology, 35(1), 94-113. doi: 10.1177/0308275X14557090

Chapter 8

Meeting the Pope

The beauty of Rome helped distract the Mardons from the anxiety of what they were really there for — to meet the pope. The pope's general audience tends to be held on Wednesday's so that's when the Mardons had been scheduled to see him. It regularly takes place in St.Peter's Square, except during the COVID-19 pandemic. Tickets can be difficult to get and need to be ordered far in advance, but are free through the Vatican website. Some tickets are available at the gates but these are quickly sold out. Certain agencies have tickets available but they cost money. In order to get a spot near the front people began arriving in the early hours of the morning. Being members of the Order of St.Sylvester and having their meeting approved by the secretary of state, the Mardons were allocated specific seats near the front. This meant they were able to enjoy breakfast and get there later than most.

Before being admitted to the general audience, everyone was required to go through a security check and metal detectors. The line was long and judging from the bored expressions on many faces, it was clear people had been waiting a while. Being members of the Order of St.Sylvester neither Austin or Catherine had to go through the regular security check. They were able to show their badges and quickly pass through with a guard. It was convenient, but they did receive the evil eye from a couple of elderly nuns who'd been waiting in line much longer. While everyone else was funneled through metal railings to the metal detectors, the swiss guards walked Austin and Catherine right past them. Catherine's bag filled with a couple dozen rosaries made of metal and glass beads wasn't even checked. She joked she could' ve been carrying almost anything in there. Without being told where they were going, the security guards passed them from one guard to the next and suddenly they were in the front row, just to the left of the dais. They were about 10 to 20 feet away from where Pope Francis would sit and a huge crowd began to stretch behind them. Reality sunk in that they'd soon be meeting the pope and Austin was sure he was going to faint or throw up. When Pope Francis appeared in St. Peter's Square he was surrounded by security. Austin and Catherine had never seen anything like it. Austin said St.John Paul II's security was nowhere near as extensive. Everywhere there were swiss guards with real spears along with other regular guards. Security was heavily increased after the attempted assassination of St.John Paul II in 1981. Some news articles have claimed the guards find it difficult to protect Pope Francis even more so than St.John Paul II because he's incredibly interactive with so much of the crowd. As a second measure, there was a tall cement barrier between the crowd and the pope. It was about four feet high and was meant to ensure no one jumped over or got too close to him. From the photos the Mardons received, a person wouldn't be able to tell there was any security around the pope. It looks as though they're alone with him, but in reality the guards were six inches from the back of Austin's head.

Although Catherine's usually not comfortable in large crowds, the Mardons felt everyone around them was friendly. There was almost a tangible hopefulness that emanated from the group. Directly to their right were some workers from Argentina, they didn't speak English so the Mardons weren't able to talk to them much. Towards the back of the crowd Austin and Catherine spotted nearly 30 couples dressed in wedding gowns and tuxedos. Many couples come from all over the world to have their union blessed by the pope, something Austin feels has become much more common than it used to be. When he met St.John Paul II there was only one couple in attendance.

On his way to the dais, Pope Francis shook hands, kissed babies, and gave blessings to those who asked. He's very social so it took him about an hour and a half to get up to the front. When he reached the dais he gave a speech. It was in Spanish or Italian so the Mardons weren't able to understand it all, but a video is usually posted online translated into various other languages afterwards. After the speech he gave a communal blessing to the entire crowd. This is how the rosaries and medallions Catherine brought were blessed, as there would've been too many to have them each blessed individually. Following the blessing, Pope Francis returned to the crowd to visit with people who had physical disabilities. He spent quite a while talking to them. At one point he requested a glass of water and a man went running by the Mardons. He returned, at a run, with a glass of water on a silver tray. The Mardons thought it impressive he didn't spill a single drop while running over the cobblestones.

After patiently waiting, it was Austin and Catherine's turn to meet Pope Francis. He stopped to talk to the Argentinians beside them and then began walking towards them. It was incredibly intimidating. Austin thinks the pope recognized them from their file, Catherine in particular. He spent a total of about ten minutes talking to them. In hindsight, Austin wishes he would've known beforehand that Pope Francis doesn't speak English well, because he would've tried to learn some Spanish. He fluently speaks Spanish, French, Italian, German, and a few other languages, but not English. There wasn't a translator there to help them either. Fortunately, Catherine knows some Spanish. Sometimes she can speak and understand it, but sometimes she can't. Because of her brain injury, there are certain things she knows, like Spanish, that come and go. It's as though it's there, but she can only find it at certain times. Luckily, on this particular day she was able to speak quite fluently. It was a miracle! Pope Francis was jovial and good natured. Austin's fears had been for nought. He was similar to St.John Paul II but much more friendly. Catherine talked to him about the boys and their FASD and he seemed to understand what that was. He became serious when she brought it up and said it must be challenging for them. She agreed it was difficult for the boys as well as for Austin and Catherine as caretakers, even in a more developed country like Canada. At that point the pope looked at her in a way that seemed to show he understood what she meant. The Mardons then asked him to pray for them and he said he would if they prayed for him. They also talked a bit about where they were from. The Mardons then gave Pope Francis the books they'd brought with them. He saw the cover of Gandy and the Man in White and asked if it was about him. The Mardons told him yes and then he began to leaf through it. He was confused by the Cree book because he couldn't figure out what language it was. He tried reading it but said he couldn't understand. Catherine tried to explain in Spanish and Pope Francis was able to understand that it was an Indigenous language of sorts. He thought it was really interesting. Austin doesn't think the pope's read all of the books because he'd need them translated and finding a Cree translator in Italy would likely be a difficult task.

Traditionally when people meet the pope they kiss his ring as a sign of respect and love, not just for the pope but for the Catholic Church. The Italian term is "baciamano" which literally means "hand kiss". It's common to also kiss the hands of bishops and priests. It's not required, but Austin chose to kiss Pope Francis' ring. Austin says it seemed like he didn't like it as he pulled his hand away quickly. A few weeks after they were there the pope actually swatted a woman's hand after she attempted to kiss his ring. There are quite a few videos of him rebuffing other peoples' attempts. Rumor has it that he's not the first pope to dislike this tradition. Both St.John Paul II and Pope Benedict XVI apparently didn't like it either. When asked about pulling away from people trying to kiss his ring, Pope Francis said it was because he didn't want to spread germs. Due to COVID-19 he's likely to get his wish, making Austin one of the last Canadians to kiss the pope's ring. The particular ring that's usually kissed is called the Fisherman's Ring because it's most often made with an image of St. Peter who was a fisherman. The ring was originally designed as a seal to be used for wax sealing any important document. It ensured documents weren't tampered with or opened until they reached the right person. This isn't needed as often anymore because communication has become more digitized, making wax seals less common. Although not needed as often, each pope receives their own custom ring which is destroyed upon their death. This is meant to hinder fraudulence. Because it's used less often the pope doesn't always wear the fisherman ring and at times wears other rings. Austin couldn't quite recall what the ring looked like because it all happened so swiftly.

Later in the day the Mardons were interviewed. Catherine isn't a big fan of interviews, but Austin soaked it in. They were interviewed by a Canadian newspaper and EWTN, a global catholic news network based in the United States. They also had an article published in the Lethbridge Herald about them, which is Austin's home town. Later on there was a video and article made about them and used in the Edmonton archdiocese paper. Austin and even Catherine are thankful their experience is documented, so that even if they forget, it'll always be there.

Pope Francis waves at the crowd as he steps up to the dais.

Pope Francis giving his speech at the general audience.

Catherine and Austin giving Pope Francis their book, 'Gandy and the Man in White.'

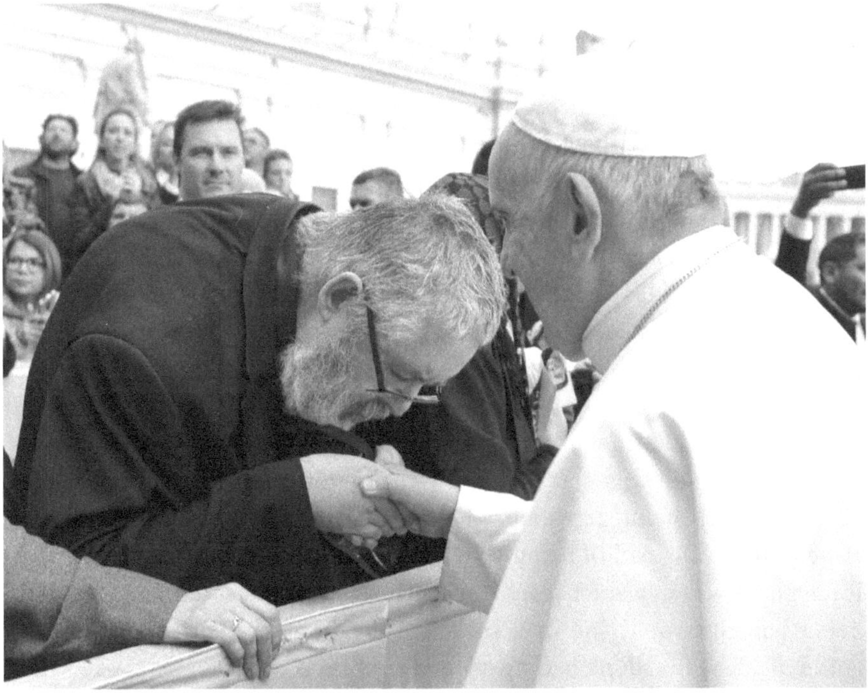

Austin kissing Pope Francis' ring.

Chapter 9

Returning Home

On their last day in Rome, the Mardons enjoyed their time relaxing and strolling around St.Peter's Square. They stayed up late that night to soak in every last bit of the city and then headed to the airport early the next morning. There was another general audience the day they were leaving which complicated things. Cars typically aren't allowed inside the square during the general audience because of the crowds of people. The Mardons had to get special permission to have a van come into the area and stop at the hotel to pick up them and their luggage. They loaded everything into the van and left for the airport. Catherine was still nervous about the flight, but felt slightly better having already gone through it once.

Upon returning home, the Mardons were exhausted from all of the excitement of Rome, but at the same time they felt relaxed. The trip had given them the ability to take a break from the stresses of their daily lives. Although they'd done a lot of walking and sightseeing, they did so leisurely, at a pace they wanted to. It was a welcome change from their normally busy schedules. Austin and Catherine are grateful to be a part of their foster sons' lives but at times it can be challenging. While they were in Rome, their adopted son was arrested and went to jail. With the time difference, he was actually being arrested right as Catherine and Austin were meeting Pope Francis. Instead of being upset, they saw it as somewhat of a miracle. It meant he was in a safer place during the cold winter months, rather than being homeless or living in a shelter. They went to visit him when they got home. The Mardons had also left one of their adult foster sons at their home while in Rome. A friend of theirs came to check in on him twice a day, but they weren't convinced the apartment wasn't going to be flooded when they got home. Thankfully he survived and so did the house. Their foster son was excited for them to return and even went to the airport to greet them. Their puppy Ollie though, was perhaps the most eager to see them. The next day when they picked him up from doggy daycare he was jumping all over them. Although sad to have left the leisurely pace and beautiful sights of Italy, it was a wonderful welcome home.

Returning from Italy, the Mardons also felt they'd further bonded and strengthened their marriage. It was the first vacation they'd ever taken together and each of their first vacations in over 15 years. Travelling often presents an opportunity to strengthen or weaken a relationship, as there are many unforeseen problems that tend to arise. Austin says their main argument was him being overly protective of Catherine. He worried about her over exerting herself and being in pain, while she just wanted to do as much as she could. Austin's paranoia also caused some challenges. Catherine often had to reassure him that they were safe, although this is something she's grown used to over their years together. Money was another struggle. Staying in such close proximity to St.Peter's Square was beautiful, but the area is also one of the more touristy which means the prices of things are greatly inflated. Expenses were a big concern for Austin and Catherine because they'd been on a fixed income for years. Both Austin and Catherine are on AISH - Assured Income for the Severely Handicappeded. AISH is a program funded by the Canadian government that provides an income for people who are unable to work full time due to having a permanent disability. It isn't a lot of money so Catherine and Austin have to be wary of what they're spending. They often thrift and buy second hand in order to help save money.

Austin and Catherine agreed they'd like to return to Rome one day. Next time Austin would like to be able to go out of the square more often to explore other parts of the city and surrounding area. It's possible they'll join a Vatican committee in the future, that way they can go back every year. Austin was actually being considered for the committee who came out with the Accompanying People in Psychological Distress in the Context of the COVID-19 Pandemic: Members of One Body, Loved by One Love document previously mentioned. He wasn't chosen this time but he plans on trying again. In order to get on a committee, a person has to be nominated by their bishop. If the Mardons do go back to Italy, they'd also like to see Pompeii. Pompeii is an ancient Roman city that was covered by the eruption of a nearby volcano, Mount Vesuvius. Although abandoned, the city was well preserved and has become a historical site. People can walk around it and explore what life was like in ancient Rome. Unfortunately, many of the roads and paths are cobblestone which makes it inaccessible for a lot of people. Currently walkers and wheelchairs aren't allowed at the site, making it impossible for Austin and Catherine to go. They're holding out hope that places like this will become more accessible by the time they return. Austin would also like to see the Appian Way either by car or on foot. The Appian Way is one of the oldest intact roads in the world and was one of the most important military and economic roads in ancient Rome. Italy is filled with countless historical sites and beautiful cities that the Mardons would love to continue exploring.

Austin and Catherine received a lot of questions about their trip when they returned. Most often they were asked what Pope Francis was like. Even people who weren't religious were interested in knowing more about him. In a way he's like a celebrity, people see him as somewhat mysterious and unlike a regular person. The rosaries and St.Christopher medals they brought back were much appreciated by everyone, even those who weren't catholic. The foster boys were happy with the medals and tokens as well, though most of them have been lost by now.

The Mardons still have the St.Sylvester medals kept in a safe location with their other awards. They haven't bought the uniforms yet because it's incredibly expensive. The knight's uniform can be upwards of $4000. Austin joked maybe if he becomes a millionaire he'll be able to afford one. They don't need it to partake in ceremonies at the church, but many order members do get it for that purpose.The Mardons haven't had the chance to participate in any yet, mainly due to the pandemic happening shortly after their induction into the order. They're looking forward to the time when they're able to do so though and will have the privilege of sitting where the archbishop and priests sit.

After returning home, Austin actually wrote Pope Francis a letter. While in Rome, the Mardons had seen a mini hospital pop up in St.Peter's Square for people who were homeless or poor. They had trailers set up for people to see cardiologists and other medical specialists, as well as ambulances to take those with more serious illnesses to the hospital. The Mardons were impressed, but noticed the makeshift hospital was missing one important speciality — psychiatry. The Mardons believe mental illness is one of the biggest issues homeless people face, so it didn't make sense not to have someone there to address it. Austin has yet to hear back from the pope. The Mardons continue to do their advocacy work for people who have a mental illness even after they received the medal and returned home.

Returning from an important trip can be difficult. It's hard to get back into the routine of regular life. When Austin and Catherine returned to Canada they were just starting to settle back into their normal lives when the COVID-19 pandemic hit. Although Canada didn't shut down until March 2021, Austin and Catherine were preparing in January. They'd seen the photos of hospitals in China and knew it was going to change everything. It was scary to realize they'd just been in the country that was seeing some of the highest case numbers. They were thankful they hadn't gotten sick but, often worried about all of the homeless people they'd seen and how they must've been affected. They listened to what Pope Francis had said about how much homeless people were suffering. Austin and Catherine tried to get some articles they'd written with the AIC students about COVID-19 in Italy published, but unfortunately they weren't picked for print. Even before a COVID-19 case was first reported in Canada, the Mardons knew the virus was going to change everything.

Chapter 10

The Pandemic and Changes to Catholic Traditions

In December 2019, the first cases of the COVID-19 virus were reported in China. It quickly spread to nearly every country in the world, becoming a worldwide pandemic. Many countries responded by going into lock downs: halting international travel, restricting gatherings, enforcing social distancing, and making face masks mandatory. Religious institutions were just one of the many groups who had to make radical changes. The Catholic Church quickly adapted to support their parishioners with mass going virtual. The changes made may be longer lasting than anticipated and the Church will need to balance their desire for community with the importance of keeping people safe.

Due to his age, Pope Francis is at high risk for contracting COVID-19 and experiencing serious outcomes from it. He and the rest of the Vatican thought it important he be vaccinated as quickly as possible. In January 2021 Pope Francis received his first dose of the COVID-19 vaccine. Shortly after, the pope came out with a statement encouraging other people to get their vaccines as well, saying it's an "act of love" to do so. The Vatican made it mandatory for staff who are able to receive the vaccine to get it. This begs the question, will those meeting the pope be expected to show proof of vaccination as well? Many countries around the world have begun adopting a policy of "vaccine passports". In simple terms, it means people need to show their proof of vaccination to be allowed into certain businesses, events, and countries. Some places are also allowing proof of a negative covid test in lieu of the vaccine passport. Italy has named it's vaccine passport a "Green Pass" and it's required to enter many businesses, including museums like the Vatican Museum. However, it isn't needed to attend mass or religious ceremonies. It's quite possible it'll be instated for the pope's general audience though, simply because of the sheer size of the crowd. Vaccines have long been controversial in the Catholic Church. Sometimes human cells are taken from aborted fetus' in the early stages of creating a vaccine, but the cells used are usually from abortions that happened decades ago and they're taken out before the manufacturing stage. In December 2020 the Congregation for the Doctrine of Faith produced a document called Note on the Morality of Using Some Anti-Covid-19 Vaccines. Essentially the documents states it's not unethical to get the vaccine because it's looking after the greater good and it doesn't mean people who get the vaccine condone abortion (Congregation for the Doctrine of Faith). The pope and all residents of the Vatican are now fully vaccinated. Pope Francis returned to holding weekly in person general audiences in May 2021, after a six month hiatus. The pope had switched to filming his weekly addresses from inside the Vatican library during the height of the outbreak in Italy rather than being out in St.Peter's Square. General audiences now have people socially distancing and are limited in numbers.

It's clear there'll be a lot of changes post COVID-19 and this includes changes within the Church. Pope Francis has never much enjoyed the tradition of people kissing his ring, luckily he likely won't have to endure it ever again. Another intimate tradition likely to be a thing of the past is shaking hands. During Catholic mass the priest calls upon parishioners to offer each other a sign of peace. Everyone turns to the people around them, shakes their hand, and says "peace be with you". It's a sign of community and goodwill towards each other. Austin thinks people will likely place their hands together in prayer and bow to each other instead, though he'd prefer to use the "live long and prosper" hand signal from the tv show Star Trek. An article from AIC actually discussed this very topic. Handshakes? Or Intergalactic Greetings? is a satirical article which discusses the meaning behind the vulcan symbol and how it actually has Jewish religious roots (Mardon et al, 2020). It'd be an interesting option to say the least. Nothing has been officially mandated by the Vatican, but many churches have encouraged their patrons to bow, make eye contact, wave, give a peace sign, or bump elbows, rather than shaking hands. Catholic mass is riddled with other close contact traditions which, although build the community, also have the potential to spread COVID-19 and other viruses. Receiving communion is one of these practices. It's one of the most important symbols of mass as it represents the last supper when Jesus broke bread and drank wine with his apostles for the last time. It's possible communion will continue as each person receives their own piece, but traditionally everyone drank from the same cup of wine. Pope

Francis encouraged parishes not to have traditional communion during the pandemic but as masses begin again and restrictions are lifted, some churches have resumed this practice. Austin thinks masks will regularly be worn both outside and inside of church for the rest of his life. He believes wearing a mask is being considerate of other people and is something that should be natural, especially when at church. It's clear not every church goer agrees with Austin. An article in the National Catholic Reporter discussed how one church was losing parishioners because some of them thought they were being too strict so they went to a nearby church (Zapor, 2021). It's a divisive issue and guidance from the Vatican may be needed to help churches know what to do.

In early 2020 as the pandemic began running rampant, many churches around the world were prohibited by their governments from having mass. During the pandemic a dispensation was given, allowing people to forego Sunday mass, but they were encouraged to attend online. The dispensation was given by bishops and as restrictions in the US and Canada begin to lift, some bishops have begun taking it away, although some members are not ready to go back yet and are questioning whether attending online is still a possibility (Boorstein, 2021). When mass went online some people attended their local service while others attended virtual masses of parishes around the world. Some stopped attending at all. As has been seen with other events and businesses, making things virtual removes a lot of barriers people face in accessing services. People may find going to online mass easier, in particular parents of young children (Zapor, 2021). Catherine's limited mobility can sometimes make physically getting to mass difficult, so this takes away that barrier as well. The Mardons believe they're not alone in this and there are a lot of other people who have disabilities or anxieties which make going to church in person difficult. Austin does think they'll go back to in person mass eventually, but it's going to take a while before they feel safe enough to do so. According to a survey in the US, a growing number of people feel it's safe to return to in person church services and an increasing number have begun to actually attend in person, although the majority of people believe some restrictions should remain in effect (Pew Research Center, 2021).

Although in person attendance has increased since last year, 58% of people who pre-pandemic attended church once or twice a month, haven't attended in the past month, and only 39% of Christians plan to go to Easter mass compared with the typical 62% (Pew Research Center, 2021). These numbers are concerning for the Catholic Church but, it's possible the pandemic has simply accelerated a decline in church going that was happening even pre-pandemic. A yearly poll in America found that for the first time in nearly 100 years there are less people that belong to a church, mosque, or synagogue than do not (Schlumpf, 2021). This gap has been happening since 2000 (Schlumpf, 2021). A quarter of people surveyed said their faith has grown stronger since the pandemic, however the majority of these were people who already had strong faith before the pandemic rather than people who were not particularly religious pre-pandemic (Pew Research Center, 2021). This could mean the pandemic has strengthened the faith of those who already had a strong base, but has decreased or not changed the faith of others. There's evidence that counters this as well though. In times of turmoil people often reach out to religion and spirituality. There's evidence this has been happening throughout the COVID-19 pandemic as words such as "prayer, god, allah, and mohammed" have been increasingly googled and people who did not consider themselves religious before the pandemic admitted to turning to prayer (Dein, Loewenthal, Lewis, & Pargament, 2020, p.4). A study completed in Italy found that people who had a member in their family who became sick with COVID-19 prayed more and attended more religious services than those who hadn't personally experienced the virus, however this was only found for those who already had at least somewhat of a religious background (Molteni et al, 2021). Austin believes he too has leaned more on his faith due to the struggles that have come with the pandemic. He feels he's become more religious and it's also created the opportunity for him to grow more in his faith by being able to go to online mass. It's difficult to predict how the pandemic will continue to affect not only the Catholic Church but other religions as well.

References

Boorstein, M. (2021). Vaccines push the question: are you going back to church? The Washington Post. Retrieved from https://www.washingtonpost.com/religion/2021/06/06/church-mass-pandemic-dispensation-lifted/

Congregation of the Doctrine for Faith. (2020). Note on the morality of using some anti-covid-19 vaccines. [Webpage]. https://www.vatican.va/roman_curia/congregations/cfaith/documents/rc_con_cfaith_doc_20201221_nota-vaccini-anticovid_en.html

Dein, S., Loewenthal, K., Lewis, C.A., & Pargament, K.I (2020) COVID-19, mental health and religion: an agenda for future research. Mental Health, Religion & Culture, 23(1), 1-9. doi: 10.1080/13674676.2020.1768725

Mardon, A., Schauer Z., Witiw, R., & Mardon, C. 2020. Handshakes? Or intergalactic greetings? [PDF]. Antarctic Institute of Canada. Retrieved from https://www.researchgate.net/publication/339946839_Handshakes_Or_Intergalactic_Greetings

Molteni, F., et al. (2021). Searching for comfort in religion: insecurity and religious behavior during the COVID-19 pandemic in Italy. European Societies, 23(Sup1), S704-S720. doi: 10.1080/14616696.2020.1836383

Schlumpf, H. (2021). Will catholics come back post-pandemic? National Catholic Reporter. Retrieved from shttps://www.ncronline.org/news/coronavirus/ncr-connections/will-catholics-come-back-post-pandemic

Pew Research Center. (2021). Life in U.S. religious congregations slowly edges back toward normal. Retrieved from https://www.pewforum.org/2021/03/22/life-in-u-s-religious-congregations-slowly-edges-back-toward-normal/

Zapor, P. (2021). What will your parish look like post-pandemic? It may depend on how it responded to coronavirus. National Catholic Reporter. Retrieved from https://www.ncronline.org/news/coronavirus/what-will-your-parish-look-post-pandemic-it-may-depend-how-it-responded-coronavirus

Conclusion

Being inducted into the Order of St.Sylvester and being able to meet Pope Francis were two of the greatest honors Austin and Catherine Mardon have ever received. It felt good to be recognized for the advocacy and volunteer work they'd been doing for over fifteen years. The award especially meant a lot to Austin because it was further proof against the people who'd said he'd never amount to anything because of his schizophrenia. Him and Catherine, both having experienced mental illness, felt receiving this award showed people that having a mental illness doesn't mean you can't do remarkable things. It was proof to their foster sons who have FASD that they too can live life to the fullest. With Catholicism and psychiatry having a complicated relationship, this award is a step towards mending it. Although the Mardons realize there is still much that needs to be done. They plan to continue working towards reconciling the two sides by giving talks to priests about the importance of mental health. They'd like to see more priests becoming educated in psychology as well as more mental health professionals being open to religious beliefs. The Mardons believe it's essential the two groups work together in order to reach struggling people where they're at. This includes providing homeless people with access to mental health care.

The Catholic Church aren't the only ones who stigmatize and discriminate against people who have a mental illness or other disability. As Austin and Catherine quickly found out, there's a lot that still needs to be done to make travelling more accessible. Although the Mardons enjoyed their time in Rome immensely, they were limited in what they were able to see. The cars weren't large enough for Catherine's wheelchair, which meant they had to rent a more expensive van. The trouble with the van was it wasn't able to go down some streets because it was too big. They of course did a lot of walking, but the cobblestone streets were difficult for Catherine to maneuver and caused damage to her walker. Some buildings and historical sites also lacked accessibility because they didn't have ramps or working elevators. Austin and Catherine would still like to return to Italy to explore more, but there would need to be improvements to make everything more accessible.

The Mardons were intrigued by the many people they saw and met in Rome. They quickly learned begging doesn't always mean someone is poor and to be wary of scammers. However, since returning home they often still think about the homeless people they saw and worry about how they fared during the pandemic. Meeting Pope Francis was a surreal experience for the Mardons. For all their nervousness, it went smoothly. The pope was friendly and took his time getting to know more about them. The Mardons hope one day they'll have the opportunity to see him again.

As restrictions begin to lift and the world adapts to living through the pandemic, the Catholic Church will potentially see a lot of changes. The Mardons predict kissing the pope's ring, shaking hands as an offering of peace, and drinking from the communal chalice will be traditions of the past. It's possible the pandemic has strengthened some folks' faith but, it's just as likely it's sped up the ongoing trend of people being less involved in religious ceremonies like mass. There's also a lot of people like the Mardons who believe virtual mass would continue to be a beneficial option for many. Although the path may not be clear, it's certain the Church will need to continue to adapt in a post-pandemic world.

Since returning from Rome Austin and Catherine Mardon have been continuing their work as advocates for those who have a mental illness or disability. After reading their story, they'd like to call people to take action in their own communities. For the Mardons, it led to international recognition, but more importantly they've shown people that small actions make big differences.

www.ingramcontent.com/pod-product-compliance
Lightning Source LLC
Chambersburg PA
CBHW030123170426
43198CB00009B/722